Grammar Girl's

101 Words to Sound Smart

MIGNON FOGARTY

ST. MARTIN'S GRIFFIN ⚥ NEW YORK

For the writers who have already used these words well,
and those who hope to in the future

GRAMMAR GIRL'S 101 WORDS TO SOUND SMART. Copyright © 2011 by Mignon Fogarty. All rights reserved. Printed in the United States of America. For information, address St. Martin's Press, 175 Fifth Avenue, New York, N.Y. 10010.

Grammar Girl is a trademark of Mignon Fogarty, Inc.

www.stmartins.com

Book design by Meryl Sussman Levavi

Illustrations by Arnie Ten

Library of Congress Cataloging-in-Publication Data

Fogarty, Mignon.
     Grammar Girl's 101 words to sound smart / Mignon Fogarty.—1st ed.
          p. cm.
     ISBN 978-0-312-57346-1 (alk. paper)
     1. Vocabulary.   2. English language—Usage.   3. English language—
Terms and phrases.   4. English language—Errors of usage.
I. Title.   II. Title: 101 words to sound smart.
     PE1449.F558 2011
     428.1—dc23

                                                        2011026115

First Edition: November 2011

10 9 8 7 6 5 4 3 2 1

Grammar Girl's

101 Words
to Sound Smart

Also by Mignon Fogarty

Introduction

It's a presumptuous task to choose 101 words that "smart people" use. Who says what's smart? What's the difference between a well-crafted sentence and a pompous sentence? How could you possibly choose just 101 words? These were the thoughts on my mind as I began this book.

I started with a long list of candidates, and the words that were easy to reject helped clarify in my mind the types of words I should include. For example, I considered *ligature,* but it was too obscure; *banal,* but it seemed too easy; *catholic,* but the secular use is too easily lost or misinterpreted among the mountain of religious uses; and *quotidian,* but every use I could find seemed unnecessary and pretentious.

Many of the words that made the cut are at least familiar to most people, but convey an especially deep meaning when the reader has an understanding of history (*Machiavellian, bowdlerize, Rubi-*

Introduction

con), different cultures (*Talmudic, Sisyphean, maudlin*), or philosophy (*existential*). The words are also general enough that most
prolific writers could find a reason to use them on occasion.

In his essay "Politics and the English Language," George Orwell
wrote, "Never use a long word where a short one will do," and
it's generally good advice, but sometimes, the short word *won't*
do. Sometimes the five-dollar word really does add a nuance
you can't get with a short word. In many cases, the words in this
book provide extra layers of meaning over more common, similar words.

Limiting the words to 101 turned out to be the challenge I
couldn't overcome. That's all we get! I would never argue that
these are the *best* 101 words smart people use or the *definitive list*
of "smart person" words, but I believe they are an excellent start.
If you master these words, you're well on your way to sounding
like a master of the English language.

Abjure

Abjure and _jury_ both share the Latin root for "swear." Whereas a jury swears an oath, to _abjure_ is to swear something off, to forswear it. _Abjuring_ can be a formal act sealed by an oath, or an informal act similar to recanting a statement or shunning a person or activity.

> **"I abjure you," Alcide said. Colonel Flood winced, and young Sid, Amanda, and Culpepper looked both astonished and impressed, as if this were a ceremony they'd never thought to witness. "I see you no longer. I hunt with you no longer. I share flesh with you no longer."**
>
> —Charlaine Harris in the Sookie Stackhouse
> novel _Dead to the World_

> **I have from an early age** abjured **the use of meat, and the time will come when men such as I will look upon the murder of animals as they now look upon the murder of men.**
>
> —Leonardo da Vinci

Anachronism

The root of **ana<u>chron</u>ism** is the Greek word *khronos*, which means "time." You'll find the same root in other "time" words such as *chronology* and *chronographer*. *Anachronism* literally breaks down to "against time," and we use it to describe something that is out of place in time, usually something that seems old fashioned. For example, some young people in

Britain believe their monarchy is an *anachronism*, that it is an out-of-date institution without much relevance in the modern world.

> **Since the arrival of container ships in the 1960s, with their need for giant cranes and open acres of wharfage, the 43 deepwater "finger piers" of San Francisco's northeastern waterfront have largely become an** anachronism. **No longer used for cargo, some serve cruise ships, ferry boats and tour boats; others have taken on new, nonmaritime uses.**
>
> —David Littlejohn writing for
> *The Wall Street Journal*

Anathema

Anathema comes from a Greek word describing something that was cursed or devoted to evil, and later, in Latin, *anathema* was associated with excommunication. For example, in the 1200s, the Catholic Church enacted various levels of excommunication and the most severe—cutting a person off from God and the Church, proclaiming him damned—was also called anathematization. The curse read during the excommunication ceremony was called the anathema.

Today, something that is *anathema* is hated, repulsive, or cursed—the epitome of evil.

> **Elizabeth Warren, the Harvard law professor and consumer advocate who is currently a special adviser to the president, is charged with setting up the [consumer finance protection] bureau. She remains a hugely popular figure among many Democrats and** anathema **to many Republicans.**
>
> —Deborah Solomon writing for
> *The Wall Street Journal*

Anodyne

Anodyne comes from a Greek word that means "painless," and it was originally used in English to describe a drug or treatment that eased pain such as opium, liquor, or herbal remedies.

Today, it is more commonly used as an adjective that carries of sense of sedating, soothing, or bland comfort.

> **"Musica + Alma + Sexo" was an opportunity for [Ricky] Martin to redefine his two-decade career for American audiences, and demonstrate that he is much more than the goofy pop singer who scored several** anodyne **crossover hits at the turn of the millennium.**
>
> —Tris McCall writing for
> *The Star-Ledger* (New Jersey)

> **There was something soothing and alienating all at once about the** anodyne **upper-middle-class blandness of the neighborhood.**
>
> —Kirsten Tranter
> in *The Legacy*

Atavistic

Atavistic comes from the Latin word for "ancestor." Its meaning is close to *primitive*, with a dash of *resurgence* thrown in. Something primitive has always been primitive, but an *atavistic* emotion is something primitive that surfaces even though people believed they had overcome or lost it.

> **I might have come away from the annual [Super Bowl] experience howling in the streets for my avenged Jets, had not my viewing been sullied by an** atavistic **rash of misogynistic commercials.**
>
> —Edward Champion writing for *Reluctant Habits*

> **That is the political imperative that drives China's exchange-rate policy right now, regardless of how much** atavistic **chest thumping comes out of Washington.**
>
> —Paul Maidment writing for *Forbes*

Avant-garde

Avant-garde sounds foreign, and it is: it comes to English from French words that mean "advance," "before," or "front" and "guard": the *avant-garde* is the group on the forefront. You're *avant-garde* if you're on the cutting edge of your field and always trying new things. Anyone can be *avant-garde*, but the term is often applied to creative types.

> **[Morton Subotnick's] wife, Joan La Barbara, is a celebrated** avant-garde **vocalist whose repertoire includes pioneering work with experimental techniques like ululation and circular singing.**
>
> —Andy Battaglia writing for
> *The Wall Street Journal*

Avant-garde work isn't always popular; to some, *avant-garde* art can seem contrived or weird just for the sake of being weird.

> **Now, before you make a movie, you have to have a script, and before you have a script, you have to have a story; though some** avant-garde **directors have tried to dispense with the latter item, you'll find their work only at art theaters.**
>
> —Arthur C. Clarke in *2001: A Space Odyssey*

Vanguard comes from the same French roots as *avant-garde* and means the same thing.

Bailiwick

Bailiwick comes from Old English words that meant "bailiff" and "village." The *bailiwick* could have been the overseer of the village, but today *bailiwick* has come to mean "one's domain." Most often, a *bailiwick* is someone's metaphorical domain—his or her area of expertise:

> **[Sam] Olens, however, clearly understands the fine line between legal advice—his** bailiwick**; and policy—not his concern.**
>
> —Bob Barr writing for
> *The Atlanta Journal-Constitution*

Occasionally, *bailiwick* is still used to describe a physical region, such as a city:

> **New York, like any town, has a right side and a wrong side of the tracks . . . and if you cross 'em, and you don't belong, suddenly your suit doesn't fit, your necktie's the wrong color and you wish you had your shoes shined that morning— things that you never cared about in your own** bailiwick**.**
>
> —Darren McGavin playing Mike Hammer
> in the TV show *Look at the Old Man Go*

Bedlam

Bedlam is the shortened name of the Hospital of St. Mary of Bethlehem, the first known insane asylum, which was established in London in the 1300s or 1400s and is known today as the Bethlem Royal Hospital. In its early years, Bedlam was known for its poor treatment of patients and the chaos and lunacy within its walls. Thus, the word *bedlam* came to mean something out of control, chaotic, loud, and noisy. For example, *bedlam* can break out in a bar once a fight gets started, during a fire when people flee hysterically, or at a town hall meeting when citizens shout down a politician.

> **The concept of dreaming is known to the waking mind but to the dreamer there is no waking, no real world, no sanity; there is only the screaming** bedlam **of sleep.**
>
> —Stephen King in *Rose Madder*

Besmirch

Smirch was a Middle English word that meant "to soil" and the *be-* prefix means "all over" or "all around." **Besmirch** combines those meanings to give us "to sully or to make dirty," which can be used in the literal sense to describe something wholly dirty or in the metaphorical sense as in describing a sullied reputation.

Men are nicotine-soaked, beer-besmirched, whiskey-greased, red-eyed devils.

—Carry Nation, American temperance activist

[Jane] Curtin said John Belushi didn't think women could write funny and he did his best to sabotage their efforts. . . . Online headlines are asking whether Belushi was a misogynist, and that's not really the point of Curtin's comments. This wasn't said to besmirch **a dead man's reputation. Curtin, 63, was trying to tell the audience that things were different then.**

—Sue Ontiveros writing for the *Chicago Sun-Times*

Bona Fides

Bona fides is Latin for "good faith." In English, it has come to mean "credentials" or "experience." When you mention *bona fides*, you're establishing someone's legitimacy in an area such as art or policy.

> **[Eddie] Jobson and [John] Wetton have impressive classic and prog-rock** bona fides, **claiming membership between them in King Crimson, Jethro Tull, Roxy Music, Asia, and Frank Zappa's band.**
>
> —Jeremy Eichler writing for *The Boston Globe*

> **[Charter schools] continue to have some high-profile flops, but in general they've made headway in establishing their** bona fides **as a K-12 alternative, and the enthusiasm they generate among many parents and students is impossible to deny.**
>
> —*San Diego Union-Tribune* Editorial Board

King
Crimson

Jethro Tull

Roxy Music

Asia

Frank
Zappa's
band

Bowdlerize

To **bowdlerize** is to "clean up" a manuscript by deleting or changing offensive words and passages, to expurgate or prudishly censor.

We get the word from Dr. Thomas Bowdler and his sister Harriet who lived in repressive eighteenth- and nineteenth-century England and decided to make William Shakespeare's scandalous plays fit for the delicate sensibilities of English ladies. Their collection of censored works was called *The Family Shakespeare: In Ten Volumes; In Which Nothing Is Added to the Original Text; But Those Words and Expressions Are Omitted Which Cannot with Propriety be Read Aloud in a Family.*

I acknowledge Shakespeare to be the world's greatest dramatic poet, but regret that no parent could place the uncorrected book in the hands of his daughter, and therefore I have prepared the *Family Shakespeare*.

—*Thomas Bowdler*

John Nance Garner, FDR's first vice-president, famously said the job of second-

in-command wasn't "worth a warm bucket of spit." Well, that's not exactly what Garner said, but in an era before "hot microphones," newspapermen were kind enough to bowdlerize it for him.

—Mark Hemingway writing for
The Washington Examiner

Cacophony

Cacophony comes from root words that mean "bad sound" and describes a harsh, grating noise. Imagine fifty dogs barking at once or traders shouting bids on the New York Stock Exchange. Although a *cacophony* is usually made of many sounds, the word is singular; two collections of discordant racket are cacophonies.

> **It's like the distant chaos of an orchestra tuning up. And then somebody waves a magic wand, and all of those notes start to slide into place. A grotesque, screeching** cacophony **becomes a single melody.**
>
> —James Callis playing Dr. Gaius Baltar in the TV show *Battlestar Galactica*

Although you won't find the definition in most dictionaries, *cacophony* is also used metaphorically, for example, to describe bright and varied visual elements or jumbled thoughts.

Cacophony

**Big, bold, punchy brights are all the rage
this season: a** cacophony **of colour to help
power us through another uncertain British
year.**

—Alice Stride writing for Furnish.co.uk

Out of the cacophony **of random suffering
and chaos that can mark human life, the
life artist sees or creates a symphony of
meaning and order.**

—*Made for Goodness* by Desmond Tutu

Cipher

Cipher comes from the Arabic word for "zero, empty, or nothing." The Arabic numbers (1, 2, 3, etc.) are called *ciphers*, and a person can *cipher* (work out) a mathematics problem.

A *cipher* can also be a sign or symbol, such as the royal *cipher* adopted by a monarch, or describe characters that have no inherent meaning, but instead have a hidden meaning, such as a code written with a nonsense alphabet.

> **At one magical instant in your early childhood, the page of a book—that string of confused, alien** ciphers **—shivered into meaning. Words spoke to you, gave up their secrets; at that moment, whole universes opened. You became, irrevocably, a reader.**
>
> —Alberto Manguel in
> *A History of Reading*

A *cipher* can also be a person, often a fictional character, who is a blank slate. A *cipher* has so little personality—is such a nothing—that the readers or viewers can project their own ideas and values onto the character.

> **Sounes's biggest weakness in telling the story is his inability to give us a fresh focus**

Cipher

on the other Beatles: John seems beyond his ken, George is a bit of a dim bulb, and Ringo, the bane of all Beatles biographers, is simply a cipher.

—Allen Barra reviewing *Fab: An Intimate Life of Paul McCartney* for *Salon*

Coterie

What rap musician might call a posse and high school girls might call a clique is called a **coterie** in more proper or stuffy circles.

Coterie comes from an Old French word related to the word *cottage*. Back then it referred to a group of tenants, cottagers, who shared land. Today it refers to a close group of people who associate together and often share a common devotion, such as to a job, cause, or person.

> **No sooner are you seated in the principal's office than a** coterie **of five preschoolers arrive at the door carrying trays and asking politely for permission to enter and serve high tea.**
>
> —Chris Davis writing for *The Wilton Bulletin*

> **It is not that our legislators are ill-behaved by nature but in due course, thanks to the** coterie **that surrounds most of them, they are on a massive ego trip.**
>
> —An anonymous official quoted by journalist Umanand Jaiswal in *The Telegraph*

Curmudgeon

A **curmudgeon** is a churlish, grumpy, ill-tempered, nit-picking, opinionated, get-off-my-lawn type of person.

Most people don't want to be around a curmudgeon unless *curmudgeon* is tempered by words such as "lovable," "harmless," or "good-natured" because an unqualified *curmudgeon* is rarely happy and is always complaining. (Perhaps curmudgeons are only happy when they *are* complaining.)

Curmudgeon is one of those rare words whose origin is unknown. Some people believe the syllable *cur* may come from the word *cur,* which means a vicious dog, but others say the association is unlikely.

Call me a curmudgeon, **but I remain underwhelmed. It's not just that Google [Art Project's] interface is frustrating, or that the choice of viewing possibilities is constrained and seemingly arbitrary. It also strikes me as a classic case of not seeing the forest for the trees. Technology is getting confused with art in ways that do little to advance the cause of either.**

—Sebastian Smee writing for
The Boston Globe

Defenestrate

Have you ever wanted to throw your computer out a window? I know I have! If we did so, we'd be **defenestrating** our computers. The root of *defenstrate* is *fenestra,* which means "window" in Latin. Add the *de-*prefix and you get "out the window" or "away from the window."

> **[Charlotte] Brontë fell in love with a married man, Constantin Heger, just like Jane, but there's no evidence that Claire Zoé Parent Heger was crazy, as in the Jane Eyre story. In the tale, the crazy wife conveniently jumps from a castle window to her death, so Jane gets Lord Rochester, but in real life, Madame Heger lived on; Brontë probably wished Madame Heger would** defenestrate **herself.**
>
> —Anton Anderssen writing for *eTurboNews*

Metaphorically, *defenestrate* also means to oust someone, such as a politician or business partner.

> **I should think that CNN [and] MSNBC . . . would actually like to have the comfort of knowing that their on-air spouters and sermonizers weren't total hypocrites, and would** defenestrate **hosts who violate basic standards. But that just isn't the world we live in.**
>
> —Michael Tomasky writing for *The Guardian*

Diaphanous

Diaphanous means sheer, transparent, or translucent. It's most often used to describe delicate or see-through fabric or clothes such as dresses or gowns. For example, the knitted lace dress Kate Middleton modeled in the fashion show where Prince William first saw her has been described as *diaphanous*. Outside of sartorial uses, someone with an extremely pale complexion could be described as having *diaphanous* skin and a forest could be described as being peppered with *diaphanous* spider webs.

Diaphanous comes from a Greek word that means "to show through."

> I guess I'm just an old mad scientist at bottom. Give me an underground laboratory, half a dozen atom-smashers, and a beautiful girl in a diaphanous veil waiting to be turned into a chimpanzee, and I care not who writes the nation's laws.
>
> —S. J. Perelman in "Captain Future, Block that Kick!"

Diaspora

Diaspora comes from the Greek word for "scatter, disperse, or sow." In English, *Diaspora* originally described Jews living outside Israel, and later expanded its meaning to describe any body of people scattered outside their homeland. When referring to Jewish people, the event that scattered the Jewish people, or the communities outside Israel in which Jewish people live, *Diaspora* is usually capitalized. When it refers to other dispersed people, *diaspora* is usually lowercase.

The concept of people as a *diaspora* originates from the biblical book Deuteronomy, which calls Jews who went to live in countries other than Palestine after the Babylonian exile "a *diaspora*," a dispersion.

> **Diasporan identity holds that the "motherland" is worthy of sustained loyalty. Yet in almost any** diaspora— **whether black, yellow, brown, or white— the dispersed are far better off, at least materially, than those "back home." For most hyphenated Americans, a trip to the ancestral lands is enough to reinforce the point—assuming, that is, that there are ancestral lands to speak of. Where, after all, does one locate the home base for the "Asian"** diaspora **or the "African"** diaspora**?**
>
> —Eric Liu writing for *Slate*

Dogmatic

A **dogmatic** person steadfastly and fervently believes in a set of principles as though they are facts, and the *dogmatic* are typically closed to competing ideas.

Dogmatic comes from the same root as *dogma*—a doctrine or set of authoritative rules or principles. *Dogma* is often associated with religious beliefs; for example, that Mary was a virgin when she gave birth to Jesus is Christian dogma.

> **Just as rigid pacifists aren't credible on national defense and** dogmatic **Christian Scientists are rarely consulted on health-care policy, a politician who has made an ideological vow to refuse to even consider tax increases is not interested in reducing deficits.**
>
> —Ezra Klein writing for *The Washington Post*

> **[Lisa] Gross . . . belongs to a class of young urban homesteaders who value making and growing their own stuff, with one hand in the dirt and the other cradling an iPhone. But she is not** dogmatic **about it. "Everything has its time and place," she says, "even a bag of Cheetos."**
>
> —Scott Helman writing for *The Boston Globe*

Egregious

Egregious means "outstandingly bad." It comes from the Latin word for "flock," which seems odd until you realize that an especially bad animal, let's say a duck, would stand out from a flock. When you think of an *egregious* act, think of an outrageous duck who is ticking off all the other ducks in his flock. Maybe he's abusing the ducklings, maybe he's in charge of the flock's bread crumb 401k and he's spending it on feather fluffing, but whatever he's doing, it stands out and it's not good.

> **Whoever's in charge of my Wikipedia—all right, whoever you are—the major, most** egregious **thing in there isn't that, you know, apparently I'm bisexual and have like, twenty kids . . . the most** egregious **of all the errors is that it says I am a massive David Bowie fan. Which is true, but it is a gross omission to leave out my obsession with Prince.**

—Patrick Stump, lead singer
of the band Fall Out Boy

25

Embolden

Embolden means "to give encouragement, to make someone bold." Politicians most often use it to accuse others of *emboldening* an enemy or to express fear that some misstep will *embolden* their opponents.

> **No, no, stop, please; it will** embolden **our enemies if you applaud for me.**
>
> —Liberal comedian and talk-show host
> Bill Maher in his HBO special
> *I'm Swiss and Other Treasonous Statements*

Although *embolden* usually has a negative connotation, it can also be used to describe positive encouragement.

> **It was some time ere I could summon courage to step on the balcony—nothing could have** emboldened **me to do so but the strong conviction of my mind, that he was still alive, and that we should again meet.**
>
> —*Guy Mannering or The Astrologer*
> by Sir Walter Scott

Eponymous

Eponymous comes from Greek roots that mean "to give name." An eponym is a word that takes its meaning from someone's name. *Boycott, maverick, silhouette,* and *mesmerize* are all eponyms, their meaning coming from the name of a person.

Eponymous is also used as a synonym for "self-titled." For example, when a band gives their album the same title as the band name, as seems most common with a debut album, it's referred to as their *eponymous* album: Led Zeppelin's *eponymous* debut album, *Led Zeppelin.* The band REM made a clever play on this practice by titling one of their albums "Eponymous."

> [Martha Stewart Omnimedia executives] announced a series of changes that indicate they are backing off the Martha Stewart name to focus on non-eponymous **products.** *Everyday Food,* a monthly magazine whose circulation has risen 50 percent in the year since it was launched, will no longer carry the tag line "From the Kitchens of Martha Stewart Living." The cover of *Martha Stewart Living* itself will be redesigned to emphasize the word "Living."
>
> —*CNNMoney.com*

Ersatz

Ersatz came to English in the late 1800s from German, in which it means means "substitute" or "replacement." We use it to describe something that is artificial, synthetic, or a substandard imitation of the original: "The worst part of a gluten-free diet is the *ersatz* chocolate chip cookies."

> **I don't personally know much about how mental hospitals were used in the 40s and 50s, . . . but it would be interesting to try to learn more about that and see how much they acted as a kind of** ersatz **prison system.**
>
> —Matthew Yglesias writing on his blog *Yglesias*

> **There are so many strange and problematic aspects of the *New York Times'* ersatz paywall plan that sometimes the big and obvious one doesn't get discussed enough: it's really really *expensive*.**
>
> —Marcus Carab writing for *Techdirt*

Erudite

The Latin roots of **erudite** literally mean "not rude" or "not untrained." Today, we use *erudite* to mean "learned or scholarly," for example, the curator at the city museum may be an *erudite* student of mid-century art.

> **For more than two decades, public-radio listeners have grown accustomed to the** erudite **questioning style of *Fresh Air* host Terry Gross.**
>
> —Jonathan Berr writing for *Daily Finance*

Erudite may also carry a sense of the extreme, such as learning beyond the interests of the common man or a person who not only is learned but also has a deep love of learning.

> **[A. C. Grayling] has been working on his opus for several decades, and the result is an extravagantly** erudite **manifesto for rational thought.**
>
> —Decca Aitkenhead writing for *The Guardian*

Finally, *erudite* can imply that a piece of writing is so detailed or scholarly that it's beyond the average person. That's why some writers feel the need to qualify their use of the word to emphasize that although someone is an expert, he or she is still "one of us."

Erudite

> Once accepted as a part of The Bay Area's creative community, [Philip] Lamantia became a key player in what the popular and literary press styled "The San Francisco Renaissance." The poets involved were young, erudite but not pedantic, dynamic and, without exception, extremely good looking.

—Peter Faulkner in *Jumping the Drunken Boat*

Existential

Existential comes from a Latin word that means "to exist," and when *existential* is used in its most literal sense, it relates to being. For example, an "existential threat to our country" is something that threatens our country's continued existence. The world's stockpile of nuclear bombs is an *existential* threat to humanity.

Existential also has a meaning tied to existentialism—a branch of philosophy that deals with existence. Begun by Kierkegaard and expanded by philosophers including Sartre and Camus, existentialism deals with questions about the meaninglessness of human life and a person's individual freedom and responsibility to make his or her life meaningful in some way. For example, an *existential* crisis could be characterized by thoughts such as "I'm just one out of 7 billion people on earth. Why does my individual life have meaning?"

> **A life that partakes even a little of friendship, love, irony, humor, parenthood, literature, and music, and the chance to take part in battles for the liberation of others cannot be called "meaningless"**

except if the person living it is also an existentialist **and elects to call it so. It could be that all existence is a pointless joke, but it is not in fact possible to live one's everyday life as if this were so.**

—Christopher Hitchens writing in
Hitch-22: A Memoir

Fathom

Sailors measure water depth in a unit called a **fathom,** which is equal to six feet. As with so many units of measure, it was originally quite inexact—measured as the distance between the fingertips of a man's outstretched arms.

From this "penetrating the deep" concept that came with measuring the depth of the ocean, we got the later "to have a deep understanding of" or "to penetrate" meaning you're more likely to hear if you aren't a sailor.

> **The mind I love must have wild places, a tangled orchard where dark damsons drop in the heavy grass, an overgrown little wood, the chance of a snake or two, a pool that nobody's** fathomed **the depth of, and paths threaded with flowers planted by the mind.**
>
> —Katherine Mansfield in *The Journal of Katherine Mansfield*

> **St. John's eyes, though clear enough in a literal sense, in a figurative one were difficult to** fathom. **He seemed to use them rather as instruments to search other people's thoughts, than as agents to reveal his own.**
>
> —Charlotte Brontë in *Jane Eyre*

Feckless

There are no donuts here. I must leave!

Given **feckless**'s straightforward construction (feck-less), you'd think that someone who is *feckless* is lacking feck. And actually, you'd be right. *Feck* is simply a Scottish form of the word *effect*, and someone who is *feckless* is ineffective, lazy, irresponsible, or weak—lacking effectiveness. A *feckless* person doesn't get results.

> **Jacqueline [Wilson], who has sold more than 30 million books around the world, is promoting her new book *Lily Alone*, which is the story of a girl left to care for her three siblings when her mum goes on holiday with a new boyfriend. . . .**
>
> **"I was always interested in grey areas, when a mum is not wicked, she is just** feckless **and doesn't sort her child care issues out."**
>
> —*The York Press*

Feckless has an antonym—*feckful*—which means effective, competent, or strong, and which, sadly, is used so seldom that it isn't included in some modern dictionaries.

Fez

A **fez** is a red felt hat, shaped like a short upside-down pail or flower pot, with a tassel (usually black), attached at the center of the top, and that hangs down the side much like a tassel on a graduation cap. It has been worn primarily by men in the Middle Eastern countries such as Turkey, Egypt, and North Africa, and at times was part of the military uniform in those countries. The name comes from the Moroccan city, Fez, where the caps were originally made.

Americans are likely most familiar with the red *fezzes* worn by men in the Shriners men's fraternity or the characters Akbar and Jeff in Matt Groening's *Life in Hell* comic strip.

Perhaps the best reason for smart people to use *fez* is that it's one of the highest scoring three-letter words in Scrabble: F (4), E (1), Z (10)—at least fifteen points.

> RIVER SONG: **Right then. I have questions, but number one is this—what in the name of sanity have you got on your head?**
> THE DOCTOR: **It's a** fez. **I wear a** fez **now. Fezzes are cool.**
> —Alex Kingston playing River Song and Matt Smith playing The Doctor in the TV show *Doctor Who*

Fiefdom

In Medieval Europe, during feudal times, a fief was a region under the control of a lord. A fief was not only the land, but also everything on the land, including the labor of the serfs, who worked hard for the right to live there. Kings often granted noblemen fiefs in exchange for loyalty or military service, but fiefs could also be inherited.

Today, a **fiefdom** is an area over which someone exerts great control, and *fiefdom* still sometimes carries a sense of the royal domination that a lord had over the serfs.

> **[The FAA is] a very secretive organization. They view it as their own personal** fiefdom. **In some ways they still resent the fact that they are part of the Department of Transportation.**
>
> —Mary Schiavo, former Inspector General of the Department of Transportation, in an interview with *Time*

> **As Bravo executive vice-president, [Andy] Cohen has made his Manhattan office a mini-shrine to his burgeoning reality** fiefdom. **Scattered throughout are framed posters, pictures, and tchotchkes immortalizing a number of his greatest hits—including *The Real Housewives of Orange County, Top Chef,* and *Flipping Out.***
>
> —Ronald Grover writing for *BusinessWeek*

Flotsam

Flotsam comes from the Old English word for "float." It's what's left floating in the water after a shipwreck.

> **The two lifeboats remained on scene to ensure that any** flotsam **that might have come to the surface from the vessel did not pose a hazard to other craft in the area.**
>
> —Coastguard watch manager Andrew Jenkins
> in an interview with the BBC

Since water-soaked bits are usually worthless, *flotsam* has also come to mean "items of unimportance" or "items of little value."

> **I would pore for hours over the stalls of worn necklaces, sets of gilt spoons, sugar tongs in the shape of hen's feet or midget hands, clocks that didn't work, flowered china, spotty mirrors and ponderous furniture, the** flotsam **left by those receding centuries in which, more and more, I was living.**
>
> —Margaret Atwood in *Lady Oracle*

Sometimes you'll hear the phrase *flotsam and jetsam* to describe trinkets or odds and ends. Jetsam is also floating debris, but jetsam was thrown overboard by the crew (jettisoned) instead of created by an accident.

Gall

Gall comes to English in two separate ways. First, *gall* is an old word for liver bile, which is yellow, and *gall* comes from Latin and Greek words for "yellow." Liver bile is bitter, and *gall* can refer to a bitter fluid or bitter feelings.

> **Though I hated him with a hatred that turned my life to** gall**, I never would have raised a hand against him.**
>
> —Emily Brontë in *Wuthering Heights*

This is also the sense from which *gall* developed in America as slang for "nerve" or "impudence."

> **More offensive than my past, it seemed, was the fact I'd had the** gall **to talk about it.**
>
> —Melissa Petro, known as the "teacher hooker," writing for *Salon*

In a second incarnation, *gall* comes to English from words in older languages that described a sore spot on a horse. From this sense we get the concept of being *galled*—mentally chaffed or irritated.

> **"I take it, then, Vijay, you are still a virgin?"**

"Yes, and I find it extremely galling. When Gandhi was my age he had already been married three years."

No wonder Gandhi turned out to be a great man. When you get your love life nailed down that early, think of all the time it frees up to devote to Great Ideas.

—C. D. Payne in *Youth in Revolt: The Journals of Nick Twisp*

Galvanize

Galvanization is an electrical process that puts a zinc coating over iron or steel. The word comes from the name of an Italian scientist, Luigi Galván, who lived in the 1700s and made significant discoveries about electricity.

The *Oxford English Dictionary* lists Charlotte Brontë as the first author to use *galvanize* in the figurative sense that is common today—meaning "bring to life" or "stimulate into action as if by electricity." The sentence is from Brontë's novel *Villette:* "Her approach always galvanized him to new and spasmodic life."

> **Fear has a lot of flavors and textures. There's a sharp, silver fear that runs like lightning through your arms and legs,** galvanizes **you into action, power, motion.**
>
> —Jim Butcher in *Grave Peril*

Gestalt

Gestalt means "form, shape, or structure" in German and was introduced to English through the Gestalt school of psychology.

In both psychology and common use, *gestalt* carries the idea of a whole being more than the sum of the parts. When used outside the psychological realm, *gestalt* usually means the core, the whole, or the totality of something.

> **Early employees of Google, Facebook, and a bunch of other successful tech companies have taken a considerable part of their paydays and become angels. And it makes sense. They work in the startup economy. They understand the technology, the market, and the** gestalt **of startup life.**
>
> —Fred Wilson writing for *Benzinga*

Gossamer

If you spend much time outdoors, especially in the fall, you've seen bits of cobwebs floating through the air or tangled among leaves—these are called **gossamer**. The name is thought to come from the Middle English "goose summer" because people ate a lot of goose during the time of year when *gossamer* was common.

Fabric that resembles floating cobwebs because of its delicacy or flimsiness is also called *gossamer,* and the word can take on a metaphorical meaning to describe anything that is delicate, flimsy, sheer, or light.

> **If we were always conscious of the fact that people precious to us are frighteningly mortal, hanging not even by a thread, but by a wisp of** gossamer, **perhaps we would be kinder to them and more grateful for the love and friendship they give to us.**
>
> —Dean Koontz in *Seize the Night*

Granular

Granular comes from the Latin word for "grain" or "granule." It can be used literally to describe something grainy such as fertilizer pellets, but in business and policy discussions, *granular* often describes a fine level of detail. When you hear of discussions at a granular level, think of people breaking down a clump of sand to sort through the individual grains.

> **But, the speeches are also aimed, in part, at the reporters in attendance—the men and women who cover this stuff at the** granular **level and who play a part in whether a candidate comes out of the conference with momentum (or not).**
>
> —*The Washington Post,*
> "What to Watch for at CPAC"

Harangue

To **harangue** means to deliver a passionate, forceful, or vehement diatribe. *Haranguing* takes a long time. It can be one long session of strident scolding or a continued campaign of badgering that extends over days, months, or years. Nobody likes to be the target of *haranguing*.

> **Bay Area water agencies seem to be winning their long battle to** harangue **customers into consuming less.**
>
> —John Upton writing for *The New York Times*

A *harangue* is the material delivered by the *haranguer*.

> **[Ayn] Rand's popularity on the street is at odds with her standing in the academic world. Some critics have called her interminable, tone-deaf, blind to human reality, a writer who creates not dialogue but** harangue. **John Galt, the mysterious central figure of *Atlas Shrugged,* has a famous (or infamous) 70-page monologue in the last third of the novel.**
>
> —John Timpane writing for the *Philadelphia Inquirer*

Harrowing

A harrow is a type of rake, and originally **harrowing** described tending a field with such a tool. In Christianity, Jesus' descent into hell before he was resurrected is sometimes called the *Harrowing* of Hell.

Today, we typically use *harrowing* as an adjective to describe a terrible and painful experience. You can remember that a *harrowing* ordeal is particularly disturbing or distressing by thinking of how frightful it would be to visit hell.

> **Many of those who escaped had** harrowing **stories of being startled awake by screams and thick plumes of smoke.**
>
> —Becky Schlikerman and Carlos Sadovi
> writing for the *Chicago Tribune*

> **If you live like a goldfish, you can survive the harshest, most thwarting of circumstances. There was an infamous incident . . . published by the Goldfish Society of America—a sadistic five-year-old girl threw hers to the carpet, stepped on it, not once but twice—luckily she'd done it on a shag carpet and thus her heel didn't quite come down fully on the fish. After thirty** harrowing **seconds she tossed it back into its tank. It went on to live another forty-seven years.**
>
> —Marisha Pessl in *Special Topics in Calamity Physics*

Haughty

The root word of **haughty** is the French word for "high": *haught* (also spelled *haute* and *haut*). A *haughty* man thinks highly of himself, feels superior to others, and shows it.

> **The** haughty **and imperious part of a man develops rapidly on one of these lonely sugar plantations, where the owner rarely meets with anyone except his slaves and minions.**
>
> —Rutherford B. Hayes, American president

The same root from *haughty* gives us *haute couture,* French high fashion. Haute couture designers create high-end, custom clothes for women.

Histrionics

Histrionics comes from the Latin word for "actor," and someone who is displaying *histrionics* is acting. *Histrionics* can carry a sense of over-the-top theatrics; however, it is not related to *hysterics* in any way.

> For years now, [Nicolas] Cage has been parlaying his loose cannon charisma and credibility as an acclaimed actor into an increasingly dreadful body of work. His fans—and they are still many—argue that there is a method to Cage's cinematic histrionics, that those who criticize his unorthodox performances miss the bravery of them.

—Mary Elizabeth Williams writing for *Salon*

Hoi Polloi

The **hoi polloi** are the masses, the average people. The word comes from Greek that means "the many" or "the masses."

Hoi polloi is an interesting case of redundancy because the typical phrase in English is *the hoi polloi,* which gives it a literal double *the:* "the the many." Such redundancy isn't unheard of with foreign words. For example, *chai* is an Indian word for "tea," so *chai tea* means "tea tea."

> **It's that time of year. Wall Street firms are prepping for their annual meetings with investors, their yearly chance to rub shoulders with the** hoi polloi, **otherwise known as their stock holders.**
>
> —Shira Ovide writing for *The Wall Street Journal*

> **Few women's wardrobes have undergone the scrutiny that Kate Middleton's has received since her engagement to Prince William. . . . Yet notoriously tough critics in the fashion world, as well as the** hoi polloi, **like what they see.**
>
> —Suzanne S. Brown writing for the *Denver Post*

Imperious

An **imperious** person is domineering, overbearing, and haughty. Imagine a queen who is briefly lowering herself to notice the presence of an underling.

> The original [State of the Union] was a modest affair, in keeping with the constitutional requirement that the president give Congress "Information of the State of the Union and recommend to their Consideration such Measures as he shall judge necessary and expedient" . . . But today's SOTU has become an imperious sermon befitting an Imperial President, short on "Information," long on pomp and circumstance, and larded with exorbitant demands on the public purse.
>
> —Gene Healy writing for *The Washington Examiner*

Imperious

Imprimatur

An **imprimatur** is a metaphorical seal of approval, legitimacy granted by an authority or by association with an authority.

In Latin, *imprimatur* means "let it be printed," and it was originally used to describe printed works that were sanctioned by the Catholic Church.

> **While altruism may sound as simple as cutting a check to an appreciative cause, such efforts can be fraught with missteps. In 2010, for example, as part of a "Buckets for a Cure" promotion to raise money and awareness for breast cancer, KFC changed its fried chicken buckets from red to pink.**
>
> **Both KFC and Susan G. Komen for the Cure, which lent its** imprimatur **to the promotion and was its beneficiary, were widely ridiculed, with critics associating deep-fried chicken with obesity, and adding that among postmenopausal women obesity has been linked to an increased risk of breast cancer.**

—Andrew Adam Newman writing for
The New York Times

Inchoate

An **inchoate** idea or movement is just getting started; it's not yet fully formed.

Inchoate comes from root words that are related to hitching a yolk to a plow animal such as an ox. Think of something that is *inchoate* as a project, like plowing, that's just getting started or is about to get underway. Because an *inchoate* thought or project isn't mature, *inchoate* often also carries a sense of being ill formed, undeveloped, or rudimentary.

Though they sound similar, don't confuse *inchoate* with *incoherent*. An *inchoate* idea is comprehensible, even if it's nascent and incomplete.

> **In Egypt these are days of rage.** Inchoate.
> **Leaderless. No one knows what the mob**
> **will settle for, what society they want.**
> **There is a dangerous vacuum.**
>
> —Gavin Hewitt on his BBC blog

Interminable

The root of **interminable** is the word *terminate*, and the *in-* prefix makes it negative. Therefore, an *interminable* dinner conversation will never end—or at least, it feels that way.

> **Many of my colleagues, especially those under 35, simply don't own [a wristwatch]. When they want to know the time, they dig into a pocket and extract a phone. That's great until they're sitting in a seemingly** interminable **meeting and want to know, discreetly of course, how much more they'll need to endure.**
>
> —Steve Fox writing for *PC World*

Inure

To become **inured** is to become accustomed to a difficult situation.

> **A new study from Canada shows that Zen meditators develop altered brain structures that can actually fend off pain. It's thought that the sometimes painful postures** inure **them to the feeling.**
>
> **Having tried the Lotus position once, I can truly vouch for the pain.**
>
> —Robert McNeil writing for the *Belfast Telegraph*

Inure often carries the negative sense of becoming numb or hardened to something terrible.

> **My heart should be breaking, too, but there comes a point when you're so** inured **to loss that you no longer feel the lash.**
>
> —Ann Aguirre in *Doubleblind*

In legal circles, *inure* has a different meaning that is similar to "transfer for benefit." For example, funds may improperly *inure* from a company to the private benefit of an executive.

Jejune

Jejune comes from Latin for "empty" or "barren," specifically empty of food—"fasting" or "hungry"—and provides an example of how definitions broaden over time. From "without food" came the slight change to "lacking nourishment," which then broadened to mean "uninteresting" as in "something that provides no mental nourishment."

Today, *jejune* means not only "uninteresting," but also "dull, insipid, or intellectually thin."

> **[Ed] Miliband's speech to a union rally last month, in which he excitedly compared the campaign against cuts to that against apartheid, made him look hopelessly jejune.**
>
> —*The Economist*

To this day, the meaning of *jejune* continues to expand. Dictionaries include the definitions "immature," "juvenile," and "childish," but some usage experts object to such use because it's thought to be based on the (mistaken) belief that *jejune* is related to *juvenile*. However, the error is so common that it's becoming standard. Be cautious about using *jejune* to mean "juvenile," because some people object, and also make sure your meaning is clear; it's often impossible to tell from the context whether the writer means "insipid" or "childish."

I know it's all very frowned-upon and hopelessly jejune **to love the [White House Correspondents] dinner and look forward to it, but I have never had a bad time.**

—Julie Mason in an interview with *Mediabistro*

Juxtaposition

Juxta means "near" in Latin, and *position* means "position." When things are in **juxtaposition**, they are next to each other. In practice, things are most often described as being *juxtaposed* when we can glean some meaning from their proximity; for example, they contrast or complement each other.

There has rarely been a starker juxtaposition of evil and innocence than the moment President George W. Bush received the news about 9/11 while reading *The Pet Goat* with second-graders in Sarasota, Fla.

—Tim Padgett writing for *Time*

Kerfuffle

A **kerfuffle** is a disturbance or commotion. Perhaps because the word *kerfuffle* sounds so amusing, it often carries the sense of being a frivolous fuss. A comic suggesting that Superman might renounce his U.S. citizenship can cause a *kerfuffle*, and the first lady wearing a dress designed in Britain instead of the United States can cause a *kerfuffle*, but a robber spraying a bank with bullets causes more than a *kerfuffle*.

> **But as a skilled stand-up comedian . . . it was the humor beyond the printed page that made the session most memorable . . . [for example, Patton Oswalt's] response to a *kerfuffle* in the front row shortly after he took the stage. When two tattooed young women in black dresses scrambled out of their chairs, Oswalt responded as if they were comedy club patrons leaving a set. "Oh, go ahead, run from the truth." Then he noticed they were fleeing a bee and he started laughing.**

> —Adam Tschorn writing for the *Los Angeles Times*

Kerfuffle is more common in Britain than in the United States and comes from the Scottish word *curfuffle*. There are many acceptable alternate spellings, including *curfuffle*, *carfuffle*, *kafuffle*, and *kurfuffle*.

Lackadaisical

Lackadaisical describes someone who is lazy, lax, apathetic, or careless—a slacker. Although today it sounds high class, it has its roots in an archaic interjection that's easy to imagine coming from the mouths of street urchins.

In the late 1400s, *alack* was a word similar to *alas,* and by the late 1500s it had morphed into the interjection *lack-a-day,* which meant something like "alas, the day" or "shame on the day."

> **Like some tea-kettle sighing,**
> **My heart and liver frying,**
> **By inches I am dying,**
> **For little Cupid, E'nt it stupid? . . . Lack-**
> **a-day!**
>> —"Oh Venus! Sweet Mamma of Love" by
>> Montcrieff (recorded in *The Universal Songster*)

By the 1700s, it had morphed again—first into *lackadaisy* and then quickly into *lackadaisical,* with the shame and pity that were before heaped on the day somehow transferred to beings with less-than-industrious characteristics. *Lackadaisical* is the only form in use today.

> **Shadow opened one** lackadaisical **eye, then**
> **shut it. Jane snorted in disgust.**
>> —Emily Carmichael in *The Cat's Meow*

Languid

Languid evokes a sense of lying around, lounging, laziness, slowness, weariness, or weakness. A barely flowing river could be described as *languid*. The word comes from the same Latin root as *languish*.

> As a young child I wanted to be a writer because writers were rich and famous. They lounged around Singapore and Rangoon smoking opium in a yellow pongee silk suit. They sniffed cocaine in Mayfair and they penetrated forbidden swamps with a faithful native boy and lived in the native quarter of Tangier smoking hashish and languidly **caressing a pet gazelle.**
>
> —William S. Burroughs in "The Name Is Burroughs"

In news stories, *languid* most often describes art such as music or fictional characters.

> [Robin Pecknold's] plaintive voice is backed by a meandering guitar; the harmonies that once burst forth are dialed back, and the drums beat out a more languid **beat.**
>
> —Theo Spielberg writing for *The Huffington Post*

Louche

Louche comes from a French word that means "squinting." In English, we use *louche* to describe a person who is shifty or a business of ill repute. If the restaurant down the street isn't serving much food but has significant traffic, it could be a front for something disreputable, so you could call it a *louche* establishment.

The ballet [*Manon Lescaut*] is a superb showcase for its two leads, but also shows the acting skills of the entire company as a whole in its evocation of the louche **underbelly of 18th-century Paris.**

—Judith Mackrell
writing for
The Guardian

Lugubrious

Lugubrious comes from the Latin word for "mournful," and its meaning didn't change much in transit to English. An exceedingly mournful, bleak, or sorrowful teen is lugubrious.

> **[Edwin] Lyman is a** lugubrious **presence at every nuclear event in Washington, ruing that the technology was ever invented and predicting gloom and doom to all if it is pursued.**
>
> —William Tucker writing for *The American Spectator*

> **When [Nirvana's *MTV Unplugged in New York*] first aired . . . it served to reinforce what many of us already knew about Kurt Cobain: that his songs could be stripped down to basics without losing their innate melodies, that he had a fondness for pretty,** lugubrious **tunes, and that there was an intense, lonely vulnerability lurking behind that scraggly blond hair and those dark eyes.**
>
> —David Browne writing for *Entertainment Weekly*

Machiavellian

Like many eponyms, **Machiavellian** is an economical way to sum up the entire philosophy of one person, in this case, Niccolò Machiavélli, an Italian Renaissance political player. After being exiled from Florence, Machiavelli wrote his most famous work, *The Prince,* in which he laid out the idea that a leader must use any means necessary to maintain power and therefore survival for himself and stability for his country.

Machiavelli wrote about governance, and *Machiavellian* is commonly used to describe ruthless politicians, but its realm has expanded to include anyone who uses cunning or deceit to maintain power without regard for ethics or morality. Famous Machiavelli quotations include "It is much safer to be feared than loved," and "A prudent ruler ought not to keep faith when doing so would be against his interest."

I miss them already. The factions, the vendettas, the Machiavellian **jockeying for pathetic scraps of power as a dying Labour government wastes its last days in office. I'm talking, of course, about the assorted villains and hapless timeservers in Armando Iannucci's satirical TV show *The Thick of It.***

—Jonathan Jones writing for *The Guardian*

Maudlin

Maudlin people are weepy, emotional, or gushily sentimental. Maudlinness can be someone's general disposition or can be brought on by alcohol or an emotional situation.

Maudlin was first used in the early 1500s, and we get the word from the biblical character Mary Magdalene. In medieval art, Magdalene was almost always shown weeping, either washing Jesus' feet with her tears or weeping outside his empty tomb. People of the time referred to anyone who had a similar weepy look or disposition as *Magdalene*. Over time, the pronunciation became slurred and the spelling changed to *maudlin*.

> **Alcohol is perfectly consistent in its effects upon man. Drunkenness is merely an exaggeration. A foolish man drunk becomes** maudlin**; a bloody man, vicious; a coarse man, vulgar."**
>
> —American frontier author Willa Cather in "On the Divide" for *The Overland Monthly*

Mesmerize

The term **mesmerize** comes from the name of Franz Anton Mesmer, a German doctor who lived in the 1700s, supported musicians, including Mozart, and came up with the concept of animal magnetism.

Mesmerize means to hold someone in your thrall, as if they are hypnotized or spellbound.

> **Before you become too entranced with gorgeous gadgets and** mesmerizing **video displays, let me remind you that information is not knowledge, knowledge is not wisdom, and wisdom is not foresight. Each grows out of the other, and we need them all.**
>
> —Arthur C. Clarke

Dr. Mesmer developed a technique for healing people that he originally thought was the result of magnetic fields and an invisible fluid that surrounded all living things. He discovered that magnets weren't necessary and concluded that certain people had "animal magnetism" that allowed them to influence and heal others. Although his treatments were popular, officials proclaimed him a fraud and he moved to Paris, where he also practiced *mesmerism,* but was again dogged by controversy.

Recognizing that *mesmerism* results were actually effected by patients' own minds, one of Mesmer's students went on to develop and promote hypnosis.

Milquetoast

Milquetoast comes from the name Caspar *Milquetoast,* a character created in the 1920s by H. T. Webster for his *Timid Soul* comic strip. Mr. *Milquetoast* takes his name from the American breakfast dish milk toast, in which toast is soaked in a mild white sauce. A mild-mannered, timid soul can be called "a *milquetoast,*" and *milquetoast* is also used as an adjective to describe someone who is bland, meek, and unthreatening.

> **"Progressives," today's** milquetoast **substitute for old-line radicals, have trembled at [Glenn Beck's] ravings about the left's conspiracies against freedom.**
>
> —Alexander Cockburn writing for Creators.com

> **There were exceptions in this generation of cars, they admit, but the generic engines,** milquetoast **styling and ubiquitous plastics made the cars as disposable as $29 DVD players.**
>
> —Bobby Cramer writing for the blog
> *Bark Bark Woof Woof*

Misanthrope

Misanthrope shares its Greek root *anthrōpos* with the word *anthropology*. *Anthrōpos* means "people or mankind." Whereas an anthropologist studies people, a *misanthrope* hates people.

Whenever I tell people I'm a misanthrope they react as though that's a bad thing, the idiots. I live in London, for God's sake. Have you walked down Oxford Street recently? Misanthropy's the only thing that gets you through it. It's not a personality flaw, it's a skill.

It's nothing to do with sheer numbers. Move me to a remote cottage in the Hebrides and I'd learn to despise the postman, even if he only visited once a year. I can't abide other people, with their stink and their noise and their irritating ringtones.

—Charlie Brooker in *Screen Burn*

Nascent

Nascent comes from a Latin word that means "to be born." In English, something *nascent* still has a sense of being born— it's new or at its beginning. A *nascent* political movement is just emerging; a *nascent* career is just getting started, and a *nascent* industry is on its way but still a little shaky.

> **We are the bright new stars born of a screaming black hole, the** nascent **suns burst from the darkness, from the grasping void of space that folds and swallows—a darkness that would devour anyone not as strong as we.**
>
> —Dave Eggers in
> *A Heartbreaking Work of Staggering Genius*

Neologism

Neologism comes from *neo*, which means "new," and *logos*, which means "word." *Neologisms* pop up every day. To give just a few examples, *neologisms* are created by

- **blending existing words (combining parts of *spoon* and *fork* to get *spork*)**
- **reusing a common ending (*alcoholic* leading to *workaholic* and *shopaholic*)**
- **pronouncing the letters of an abbreviation as a word (*L.A.S.E.R.* leading to *laser*)**
- **assigning a meaning to a person's name (*Orwellian* and *pasteurize*)**
- **pulling meaning from thin air (*blizzard,* an Americanism first used in 1825)**

The children's book *Frindle* by Andrew Clements tells the story of ten-year-old Nick Allen who creates the *neologism frindle*—his new name for a pen—and eventually gets the word included in the dictionary.

> **Adapt your style, if you wish, to admit the color of slang or freshness of** neologism**, but hang tough on clarity, precision, structure, grace.**
>
> —William Safire writing for *The New York Times*

Nonplussed

Nonplussed is used often, but smart people use it properly—it means to be confused, perplexed, or at a loss for words. For example, you can be left *nonplussed* by behavior that is so outrageous you don't know what to say or by someone's statement that is so off-the-wall you don't know what it means.

Nonplussed comes from Latin *non* meaning "no" and *plus* meaning "more" and got its current meaning from the idea that when you're *nonplussed,* you're in a situation where you're left speechless—there's <u>no more</u> to say.

An audience was left cold when a psychic's attempts to contact the dead flopped.

Medium Simon Lock ended up asking his nonplussed **audience if the names "Dave" or "Mike" meant anything to anyone. . . . Our source said: "Then he started asking if anyone had a connection with a brown dog or black cat—but nobody said anything."**

—Stian Alexander writing for
Daily Star

SQUIGGLY WENT TO THE STORE? I ALREADY PICKED UP EVERYTHING WE NEED!

Nuance

Nuance comes from a French word that means "shades"—specifically, small differences in shades of color.

In English, a *nuance* is a subtle difference. You can think of it as shades of meaning, taste, color, or feeling with only slight differences, just as there is a slight difference in color between fern and forest green crayons. Whereas the typical person may barely be able to tell the difference between two types of Cabernet, a connoisseur will be able to identify the many nuances of flavor.

> **A man with a scant vocabulary will almost certainly be a weak thinker. The richer and more copious one's vocabulary and the greater one's awareness of fine distinctions and subtle** nuances **of meaning, the more fertile and precise is likely to be one's thinking. Knowledge of things and knowledge of the words for them grow together. If you do not know the words, you can hardly know the thing.**

> —Henry Hazlitt in *Thinking as a Science*

Obduracy

Obduracy is stubbornness, obstinance. *Obduracy* shares its Latin "dur" root, which means "hard" or "to harden," with the words *durable* and *endure*. When people are exhibiting *obduracy*, they are hardened to their position or course of action.

> **There may be admirable aspects to the** obduracy **of a candidate who refuses to be broken to the saddle of campaign discipline, but there also may be arrogance—and the laziness of someone who is indefatigable when doing what he enjoys, but only when doing that.**
>
> —George Will writing for *Newsweek*

Obduracy sometimes carries the sense that a person is unbendingly pursuing something evil or immoral.

Obsequious

Obsequious people are more than attentive; they're servile and fawning. "Yes, sir," an *obsequious* waiter may respond as he leaves the table with a slight bow. "Oh, no. Let me get that for you, ma'am," an *obsequious* boutique clerk may purr as she offers to take a customer's bags to the car. *Obsequious* also sometimes carries a sense of insincerity. For example, flatterers and social climbers can be *obsequious* for their own purposes.

Obsequious comes from a Latin word whose root means "to comply."

> **Those who talk about the "good old days" of flying refer to gourmet meals on fine china in the sky,** obsequious **flight attendants who catered to the passenger's every whim, and seats the size of a '57 Chevy's throughout coach.**
>
> —Alex Resnik writing for *NileGuide*

Occam's razor

Occam's razor (also spelled *Ockham's razor*) is a phrase that means the simplest solution is usually the right one. For example, if you find a basket of tomatoes outside your door, it's conceivable that ninjas are trying to poison you because, although you don't know it yet, you are essential for their enemy's evil plan; but *Occam's razor* suggests it's more likely your neighbor who likes to garden, and gave you tomatoes last year, left them there.

A fourteenth-century Franciscan monk and philosopher, William of Occam, gives us the *Occam* part, and it's called his razor because the idea is to shave away complexity.

Although William heartily subscribed to the theory we now call *Occam's razor* and used it often in his writings and debates, philosophy scholars say the idea existed well before him and it isn't stated as succinctly in his writings as we think of it today.

> **All conspiracy theories fail** Occam's razor.
> **Never attribute to malevolence what can be**
> **explained by incompetence.**
>
> —Commenter "yellojkt" on
> the Washington Post blog

Omertà

The **omertà** is the mafia oath of silence that members take during the ceremony in which they are "made." Today, it can be used to describe any conspiracy of silence.

It's origin is uncertain, but *omertà* may come from the Sicilian word for "manliness."

> **In accepting money for their clandestine trade [prostitutes] are surely bound by a code of** omertà**. The unwritten deal between client and prostitute is that the sex will remain secret.**
>
> —Roy Greenslade writing for *The Guardian*

Pedantic

A **pedantic** person is smart, wants you to know it, and often explains things in unnecessary detail. He may dwell on the Latin names of plants at a garden party or explain the complete system behind frequent shopper cards while you wait in a long line. The explanations don't have to be long, they may be simply tiresome, condescending, or ostentatious.

Pedantic comes to English from French and Italian words that mean "to instruct" and probably has the same root as a word you'd hear at a teachers' conference: *pedagogy*. A pedagogy is a way of teaching, a theory or method. (*Pedagogy* doesn't have a negative connotation as *pedantic* does.)

LORD PERCY: After literally an hour's ceaseless searching, I have succeeded in creating gold, pure gold.

BLACKADDER: Are you sure?

LORD PERCY: Yes, my lord. Behold.

BLACKADDER: Percy, it's green.

Pedantic

> **Lord Percy:** That's right, my lord.
>
> **Blackadder:** Yes, Percy, I don't want to be pedantic **or anything, but the color of gold is gold. That's why it's *called* gold. What you have discovered, if it has a name, is "green."**
>
> —Rowan Atkinson playing Edmund Blackadder
> and Tim McInnerny playing Lord Percy
> in the TV miniseries *Black-Adder II*

Peripatetic

Peripatetic describes someone who is always on the move, a wanderer or itinerant traveler. If you went to six different elementary schools, you had a *peripatetic* childhood, for example.

> **[Nathan Hines] can give the impression that it's all been a bit of a hoot, this** peripatetic **career that has taken him around the world and allowed him to play professionally in three countries.**
>
> —Alasdair Reid writing for *The Telegraph*

Peripatetic comes from the name for Aristotle's school of philosophy, in which the instructor would walk around while teaching or engaging in discourse. Therefore, the word is particularly well used when describing someone who engages in intellectual activity while walking.

> **Many a middle of a night I could hear her creaking around the dead house with a pen in one hand, a clipboard and a flashlight in the other, refining her poems. . . . She never courted the muses, she wrestled them, mauled them all over the house and came up, after weeks of** peripatetic **labor, with a slim Spencerian sonnet, fourteen lines of imagistic jabberwocky.**
>
> —Millard Kaufman in *Bowl of Cherries*

Profligate

Profligate describes something wasteful, reckless, or ruinous. It shares a Latin root with the words *inflict*, *afflict*, and *conflict*.

> **It was brought home to [Müller] that unless he reformed his mode of living his success in his calling as a clergyman would be seriously at stake; but good resolutions to lead a better life were as nothing to the godless young man, and being now more than ever his own master, he renewed his profligate ways, regardless of the fact that he was a student of divinity. When his money was spent, he pawned his watch and his clothes, or borrowed in other ways.**
>
> —Frederick G. Warne in
> *George Müller: The Modern Apostle of Faith*

Although *profligate* is most often used in a financial sense, it can also describe other extravagant or spendy practices.

> **Nature is, above all,** profligate. **Don't believe them when they tell you how economical and thrifty nature is, whose leaves return to the soil. Wouldn't it be cheaper to leave them on the tree in the first place? This deciduous business alone is a radical scheme, the brainchild of a deranged manic-depressive with limitless capital. Extravagance!**

—Annie Dillard in *Pilgrim at Tinker Creek*

Prosaic

Prosaic means "ordinary," "unimaginative," "common," "dull," or "plain." It comes from the same root word as *prose,* from which it takes its meaning. *Prosaic* is "like prose," which is the opposite of *poetic.* Whereas poetry is exciting, creative, and full of imagination, prose is not—or so thought the people who gave *prosaic* its meaning. They must have been poets.

> **U2's Bono (**prosaic **real name = Paul David Hewson) and the Edge (**prosaic **real name = David Howell Evans) share the musical credit for "Spider-Man."**
>
> —Alex Beam writing for *The Boston Globe*

Provincial

Provincial comes from the word *province*, as in the French provinces outside of Paris. Since provinces are more rural and simple than the cities they surround, *provincial* took on a meaning reflective of country life: "unsophisticated" or "rustic."

Taking that anti-country sentiment a bit further, *provincial* has also come to describe a narrow outlook or someone who doesn't care about events beyond a narrow region: *"This place is so* provincial *nobody even considers going to an out-of-town college."*

> **Man is always inclined to regard the small circle in which he lives as the center of the world and to make his particular, private life the standard of the universe. . . . But he must give up this vain pretense, this petty** provincial **way of thinking and judging.**
>
> —Michel de Montaigne,
> French Renaissance writer, in *Les Essais*

> **Living in a foreign country is one of those things that everyone should try at least once. My understanding was that it completed a person, sanding down the rough** provincial **edges and transforming you into a citizen of the world.**
>
> —David Sedaris in *Me Talk Pretty One Day*

Purloin

To **purloin** is to take something that isn't yours. It can be synonymous with "steal," but it can also be a less severe taking—a lifting or pilfering. The emphasis is usually on the wrongness of removing the thing, not on the illegality of the thievery.

> **It is curious how sometimes the memory of death lives on for so much longer than the memory of the life that it** purloined**.**

—Arundhati Roy in *The God of Small Things*

Quagmire

Literally, a **quagmire** is soggy, soft piece of land; imagine a bog that will suck off your shoes.

> **There was a salt-marsh that bounded part of the mill-pond, on the edge of which at high water we used to stand to fish for minnows. By much tramping we had made it a mere** quagmire. **My proposal was to build a wharf there fit for us to stand upon, and I showed my comrades a large heap of stones which were intended for a new house near the marsh.**
>
> —Two-Hundredth Anniversary of the Birth of Benjamin Franklin by the Franklin Bicentennial Committee of Boston, Massachusetts

Metaphorically, a *quagmire* is a difficult, perplexing, or dangerous situation—something that may be as hard to get out of as a soggy bog.

> **American history is a** quagmire, **and the more one knows, the quaggier the mire gets.**
>
> —Sarah Vowell in *The Partly Cloudy Patriot*

Quagmire

The exact origin of *quagmire* is unknown. The "mire" part certainly comes from *mire,* which is another name for wet, muddy land; but *quag* is a mystery. It may be related to *bog* or *quake.*

When politicians talk about a situation being a *quagmire,* visualize them ankle deep in mud.

Rabble

The **rabble** is a mob of common people—the hoi polloi gone wild or a lower-class group with the potential to become disorderly. Originally, *rabble* described a pack of animals, but it quickly became applied to a pack of unruly people.

You'll most often encounter *rabble* in the compound *rabble-rouser*. A *rabble-rouser* stirs the coals, incites the mob. (It's not often used in this way in the news or in literature, but a *rabble* is also a tool for stirring the fire in a furnace.)

> **While we often think of Mom as the ultimate icon of home and hearth, not a** rabble-rouser **taking to the streets, some say we have overlooked the fact that a mother's love for her family naturally extends beyond the scope of her minivan. That's because the destiny of her children is inextricably entwined with the state of the world, from foreign policy to environmental issues.**
>
> —Karen D'Souza writing for the *San Jose Mercury News*

Repose

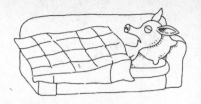

Repose means to rest, relax, or sleep; or it describes the state of someone who is resting, relaxing, or sleeping. For example, a woman in *repose* may be calm and composed or tranquil. A dead person can also be said to be in *repose*. Since *repose* can be a noun or a verb, a body can *lie in repose* (noun) or *repose in the church* (verb).

Repose comes from Latin that means "to pause" and "to stop."

> **Consider the peaceful** repose **of the sausage compared with the aggressiveness and violence of bacon.**
>
> —Tom Robbins in *Another Roadside Attraction*

> **On the shore, dimly seen through the mists of the deep,**
> **Where the foe's haughty host in dread silence** reposes,
> **What is that which the breeze, o'er the towering steep,**
> **As it fitfully blows, half conceals, half discloses?**
>
> —From the second verse of "The Star Spangled Banner" by Francis Scott Key

Retinue

Retinue comes from the Old French word meaning "to retain," and literally the *retinue* are the retained—a group of people who congregate around, serve, or work for someone of higher status.

> **You can tell a lot about musicians by how they arrive at an interview. Some come with a manager, others with a publicist. Some come with bodyguards, others with a** retinue **of hangers-on. Bruce Springsteen came alone. He drove himself from his home in Rumson, New Jersey, to the Sony Music Studios in Manhattan in his black Explorer—and arrived early.**
>
> —Neil Strauss writing for *The Telegraph*

Chaucer was one of the earliest writers to use the word:

> **To the paleys rood ther many a route . . .
> Lordes in parementz on hir coursers
> Knyghtes of** retenue, **and eek Squyers.**
>
> —Geoffrey Chaucer in "The Knight's Tale"

Ribald

We typically use **ribald** as an adjective, but it got its start as a noun—the name for a low-class person of questionable moral character or the lowliest of military men. In the Middle Ages, French royals employed a "King of the Ribalds" to deal with scurrilous people in and around the court, such as prostitutes, pimps, and gamblers.

Today, the adjective *ribald* describes someone who speaks or writes indecently or offensively, often with sexual undertones. A *ribald* man probably tells a lot of obscene jokes or crude stories. *Ribald* can also describe the statements themselves: She told a *ribald* tale.

> **The extraordinary mystique of hers made you think she lived on rose petals and listened to nothing but Mozart, but it wasn't true. She was quite funny and** ribald**. She could tell a dirty joke. She played charades with a great sense of fun and vulgarity, and she could be quite bitchy.**
>
> —From *Audrey Hepburn* by Barry Paris

Rubric

Originally, in the 1400s, a **rubric** was a set of instructions for conducting a church service. The word *rubric* is from Latin for "red ochre," and the religious works were called *rubrics* because they were written in red.

Later, *rubric* took on a secular meaning. Headings for laws and book chapters in manuscripts were written in red and called *rubrics,* and *rubric* came to mean any set of official rules, guidelines, or instructions.

> **The state provides a** rubric **for teachers to guide them about when to give a student a point for reaching certain thresholds in their answers.**
>
> —Barbara Martinez and Tom McGinty
> writing for *The Wall Street Journal*

On a related note, we call an exciting or happy day a *red letter day* because holy days were written or printed in red on church calendars.

Rubicon

The **Rubicon** was a river that defined part of the border between Italy and Cisalpine Gaul during the time of the Roman Republic. In the act that started the war that ultimately made him Emperor, Julius Caesar defiantly broke the law by leading an army across the Rubicon and advancing toward the city of Rome. From this important moment in history, "crossing the *Rubicon*" has come to mean committing to an important decision or facing a point of no return.

> **A great statesman crosses the** Rubicon
> **without considering the depth of the river.**
> **Once he or she decides to cross it, they**
> **must face any challenges and risks during**
> **the journey. Fretting on the shore won't**
> **make the dangers go away.**
>
> —Chang Dal-joong writing for
> *Korea JoongAng Daily*

Sardonic

Greeks coined the word **sardonic** from the name of the island Sardinia (now part of Italy), where a plant was said to grow that, if eaten, would force face muscles into a grimacing smile—not a smile of happiness, but a smile of pain—a *sardonic* smile. Scientists in Italy recently reported that they believe a Sardinian plant called water celery is the lethal herb the Greeks had in mind.

Sardonic means cutting, cynical, and disdainful and is often used to describe a kind of humor.

> **Why write, if everything has, in a way,
> already been said? Gide observed**
> sardonically **that since nobody listened,
> everything has to be said again. . . .**

> —*Around the Day in Eighty Worlds* by
> Julio Cortázar

Sclerotic

Sclerotic describes a belief, person, or system that has become hardened, unresponsive, or rigid over time. It comes from the Greek word for "hard" or "to harden."

For hundreds of years *sclerotic* had only medical uses, for example to describe the hard *sclerotic* coating of the eye. *Sclerotic* comes from the same root as *sclerosis*, which you may be familiar with because of the diseases multiple sclerosis (which includes hardening of some tissues in the brain and spinal cord) and arteriosclerosis (also known as hardening of the arteries).

Sclerotic took on its figurative meaning in the mid-1900s, and although this definition still isn't in some dictionaries, *sclerotic* is commonly used in the news to describe leaders, governments, and economies.

> **[Mancur] Olson concluded that, paradoxically, it was success that hurt Britain, while failure helped Germany. British society grew comfortable, complacent and rigid, and its economic and political arrangements became ever more elaborate and costly, focused on distribution rather than growth. . . . The system became** sclerotic**, and over time, the economic engine of the world turned creaky and sluggish.**
>
> —Fareed Zakaria writing for *Time*

Sedition

In government circles, **sedition** is the act of inciting discontent or a rebellion against the people or institution in charge.

Although dictionaries don't often list the more metaphorical meaning, *sedition* can also be used to describe less significant acts of undermining rebellion. For example, a financier who speaks out against the structure of the current banking system could be called *seditious,* as could a teenager who attempts to erode the influence of her clique's leader (as Lindsay Lohan's character did in the movie *Mean Girls*).

The film's seditious **theme explores the appropriation of arts and culture in the name of the almighty dollar. Everywhere, it seems, there is a mad dash for cash among artists, musicians and directors.**

Sedition

A hip-hop artist scrambles to weave a fragrance into his lyrics. A director confesses he is eager to write a cameo appearance by a certain cola into the story line.

In interviews, several prominent artists nonchalantly admit to tailoring their creations to please the product-placement people.

—Laura Washington writing about
POM Wonderful Presents:
The Greatest Movie Ever Sold
for the *Chicago Sun-Times*

Sisyphean

In Greek mythology, the gods punished the king of Cornith, Sisyphus, by condemning him to push a rock uphill only to have it roll down to be pushed up again for eternity. Thus frustrating, seemingly futile tasks that go on forever are called **Sisyphean**. The word is particularly well used if the tasks have a repetitive element to them.

> **There are a lot of prevailing myths about the Civil War . . . many of them perpetrated by southerners in their doomed quest to find some moral victory in what was, at the heart of the matter, an immoral cause.**
>
> **That** Sisyphean **quest might explain why southerners are so set on keeping the war alive, mostly through re-enacting its famous battles. You get the idea that every year, they show up at Gettysburg, thinking, "This could be our year," only to have it turn out the same every single time. They keep losing, but they keep coming back for more, perhaps out of some small hope of catching a break that would change the result—sort of like the Chicago Cubs.**
>
> —Mike Argento writing for the *York Daily Record*

Sui Generis

Sui generis is Latin for "of its own kind" and means "unique." For example, if scientists discover a species so unique that they have to assign it to its own genus, it is called *sui generis*.

You have to ask, why should I use *sui generis* instead of the less pompous-sounding *unique*? Often, you shouldn't—but *unique* has lost some of its force because of extensive misuse ("unique two-story starter house," anyone?), and occasionally *sui generis* may fit with the flow of your writing in a way *unique* does not.

> **Truly significant poets write like no one else, and David Harsent is both** sui generis **and unsurpassed.**
>
> —Fiona Sampson writing for *The Independent*

> **Some people defy comparison. I believe firmly, for example, that Dennis Johnson was completely** sui generis**. No NBA person ever—ever!—says, "This kid reminds me of Dennis Johnson."**
>
> —Bob Ryan writing for *The Boston Globe*

Talmudic

The Talmud is the book of Jewish law, and **Talmudic** describes something relating to the Talmud, such as *Talmudic* law or *Talmudic* commentary.

Talmudic scholars engage in long, hairsplitting debates about the meaning of passages in the Talmud and the application of *Talmudic* law to everyday life.

The conversation among the students irritated me: it was almost always . . . the hairsplitting minutia of Talmudic **law that animated the young Teshiva undergraduates: "Would Pepsi be kosher if it were made in a factory that was built on a former pig farm?" "What if the ground was covered with plywood before the factory was built?" That kind of thing. But the hot soup and cold weather encouraged me to dawdle and eavesdrop on some students at the next table. This time the subject of the conversation was an item that even I cared about—**

> **toilet paper! The raging** Talmudic **debate
> was over the momentous issue of whether
> toilet paper rollers may be restocked
> during the Sabbath, or whether one must
> use the paper straight from an unmounted
> roll.**
>
> —*The Black Hole War: My Battle with
> Stephen Hawking to Make the World Safe for
> Quantum Mechanics* by Leonard Susskind

By analogy to these religious debates, *Talmudic* has also taken
on a meaning that describes any painstakingly detailed analysis.

Temerity

Temerity is recklessness with a big dose of braveness mixed in. If someone has *temerity*, he or she has done something rash and bold. You'd have to have *temerity* to use the word (or non-word) *irregardless* in a room full of grammarians, for example.

> **Anyone who has the** temerity **to write about Jane Austen is aware of [two] facts: first, that of all great writers she is the most difficult to catch in the act of greatness; second, that there are twenty-five elderly gentlemen living in the neighbourhood of London who resent any slight upon her genius as if it were an insult to the chastity of their aunts.**
>
> —Virginia Woolf writing for *Athenaeum*

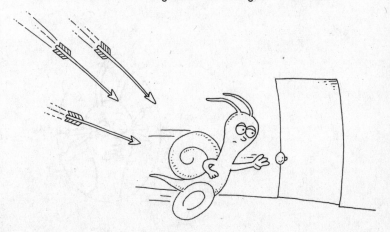

Timorous

Timorous comes from the Latin word for "fear" (as does the related word, *timid*) and the suffix *-ous,* which means "filled with" or "having the qualities of." Therefore, a *timorous* person is filled with fear.

> Once when Stonewall Jackson planned a daring attack, one of his generals fearfully objected, saying, "I am afraid of this" or "I fear that . . ." Putting his hand on his timorous subordinate's shoulder, Jackson said, "General, never take counsel of your fears."
>
> —Norman Vincent Peale in
> *The Power of Positive Thinking*

Travesty

Travesty is often used to mean simply "awful," but it has a more specific meaning. It is a mockery, a ruse, or a burlesque.

Travesty comes from French and Italian words that mean "to disguise" and, earlier, from the Latin root for "clothes." A "travesty of justice" is injustice dressed up to make onlookers believe everything is in order.

> **The real** travesty **is that universities are willing to hire people who aren't interested in their students' success.**
>
> —Keetje Kuipers, adjunct associate professor,
> University of Montana, in a letter to the editor
> of *The Atlantic*

In nonfiction, *travesty* is often used to describe a political opponent's policies or failings; but *travesty* is also a literary device that takes a serious subject or situation and makes it ridiculous. Works of *travesty* include *Don Quixote de La Mancha* by Miguel de Cervantes and *Virgile Travesty* by seventeenth-century French writer, Paul Scarron, whose popular work applied travesty to Virgil's *Aeneid* and introduced the term to England.

Truculent

A **truculent** person is fierce or savage, in action or in speech (think of a football fan made *truculent* by his team's loss). *Truculent* comes from a Latin word with the same meaning.

> **["This could not happen? But . . . but . . . but . . ."] Think of it as voiced in a** truculent **tone, as a protest; it's the response of that part of us that rejects "could not happen" as a valid objection, argues with it.**
>
> —Hal Duncan on the blog *Notes From The Geek Show*

> **Within the oftentimes bombastic and** truculent **appearance that I present to the world, trembles a heart shy as a wren in the hedgerow or a mouse along the wainscoting.**
>
> —George Moore in *Hail and Farewell*

Umbrage

Umbrage is often used as a synonym for "offense," but it is best used when it carries a sense of suspicious jealousy or hurt feelings from being slighted or wronged—a feeling that one isn't getting the attention he or she deserves. It comes from the Latin word for "shadow" or "shade," and stems from the idea of casting a shadow of suspicion on someone.

> **One of the junior new atheists—that is to say, not one of the big four of Richard Dawkins, Daniel Dennett, Christopher Hitchens and Sam Harris—took extreme** umbrage **to my picking on him ([and] even more** umbrage **at my not naming him by name).**
>
> —Michael Ruse writing for *The Huffington Post*

Occasionally, and particularly in the past, *umbrage* is also used to mean "shade."

> **She would spend a sunny afternoon in lying stirless on the turf, at the foot of some tree of friendly** umbrage.
>
> —Charlotte Brontë in *Shirley*

An easy way to remember the meaning of *umbrage* is to think of someone being thrust into the shade (and therefore out of the limelight) by a rival.

Unctuous

Unctuous comes from Latin words for "ointment" and "anoint." In religion, *unction* is still another word for "anointing." For example, during "Unction of the Sick" (today also called "Anointing of the Sick") a Catholic priest uses holy oil as part of a rite to provide healing and comfort.

In its earliest uses, *unctuous* meant "oily" or "greasy."

> **It is not, perhaps, entirely because the whale is so excessively** unctuous **that landsmen seem to regard the eating of him with**

abhorrence; that appears to result, in some way, from the consideration before mentioned: i.e. that a man should eat a newly murdered thing of the sea, and eat it too by its own light.

—Herman Melville in *Moby-Dick*

Today, *unctuous* describes a person who is insincerely ingratiating or smug, much the same way you might describe someone as "greasy" or "smarmy" (which is also related to *oily* because it comes from the word "to smear," as you would oil or ointment). *Unctuous* also describes a person who shows too much unjustified spiritual self-satisfaction.

Many religions now come before us with ingratiating smirks and outspread hands, like an unctuous **merchant in a bazaar. They offer consolation and solidarity and uplift, competing as they do in a marketplace.**

—Christopher Hitchens in *God Is Not Great*

Untoward

Untoward is simply the combination of the prefix *-un* with the word *toward*. The literal sense, not moving in the direction toward something, gave rise to the meaning "not inclined to go somewhere or do something," which gave rise to the meanings "unruly" or "difficult to control," and "unfortunate" or "annoying,"

> **If things are going** untowardly **one month, they are sure to mend the next.**
>
> —Jane Austen in *Emma*

From that common meaning in Jane Austen's time, *untoward* again evolved to convey the most common meaning we use today: "improper."

> **Harry had told her very little about his discussion with Sir Gregory: all she knew was that Tristram had been caught trespassing and that Jennifer had been caught going to meet him; but although**

each had sworn that nothing untoward **had
happened, and their reserve and good
behaviour seemed to confirm their
innocence, Ann could not forget the scandal
they had caused ten years before, nor
could she believe that Tristram would have
scaled the Roscarrock wall simply to sit
with his cousin and talk.**

—Charles Gidley Wheeler in *Armada*

In countries where English is a prominent second language,
such as India, *untoward* also commonly appears in the news to
describe actions that threaten public safety:

**Security has been beefed up in the entire
district to prevent any kind of** untoward
incident.

—*The Times of India*

Urbane

Urbane and *urban* both come from the same Latin root word that means "city." Whereas something urban is <u>of</u> the city, something *urbane* is <u>like</u> the city. At first, *urbane* just described city life or the ways of people who lived in cities, and it can still hold that meaning today:

> **The effect is a flourishing small town with** urbane **accents like the trained baristas, fresh-ingredient sandwiches and acoustic music nights with regional artists.**
>
> —Gene Stowe writing for the *South Bend Tribune*

However, *urbane* also eventually came to mean "sophisticated, refined, polite, and well mannered," presumably because city people displayed these characteristics more often than country people. Of course, *urbane* took on this meaning in the 1600s, before the existence of rush hour traffic and Black Friday sales.

> **The formal clothes should have made him look more** urbane **and civilised, but they didn't. They only served to emphasise the power and toughness which was the man beneath the civilised veneer.**
>
> —From the British National Corpus

Verdant

Verdant comes from an Old French word that meant "green." Today, a *verdant* landscape is lush, healthy, and bursting with greenery.

> [E]very couple of months Crowley would pick out a plant that was growing too slowly, or succumbing to leaf-wilt or browning, or just didn't look quite as good as the others, and he would carry it around to all the other plants. "Say goodbye to your friend," he'd say to them. "He just couldn't cut it. . . ."
>
> Then he would leave the flat with the offending plant, and return an hour or so later with a large, empty flower pot, which he would leave somewhere conspicuously around the flat.
>
> The plants were the most luxurious, verdant, and beautiful in London. Also the most terrified.
>
> —Neil Gaiman in *Good Omens*

The use is less common, but just as a novice is sometimes called green, an inexperienced or gullible person is sometimes called *verdant*.

Verisimilitude

Verisimilitude comes from a Latin word that means "like the truth." A movie, story, or proverb with *verisimilitude* rings true to the audience or to readers even though they know it is fiction.

The first part of *verisimilitude* has the same Latin root as *veritas,* which you may recognize means "truth" in Latin because many colleges use it as part of their motto; for example, Harvard's motto, *Veritas,* appears on the university seal. *Similitude* has the same root as *similar.* By noting that *similitude* sounds similar to *similar* and remembering Harvard's motto, you can easily work out that *verisimilitude* means "similar to the truth."

> **Perhaps the coolest extra material [on the *Mad Men* Season 4 disc] is the actual advertising campaign for the Ford Mustang, as well as a sort of roundup of commercials and speeches from the 1964 Presidential Campaign, which further highlight the** verisimilitude **of the show.**
>
> —Todd Gilchrist writing for *The Wall Street Journal*

> **If this is fake you've got to [give] them credit for** verisimilitude**.**
>
> —John Del Signore writing for *The Gothamist*

Vicarious

A person having a **vicarious** experience is taking a feeling—joy, pain, pleasure, satisfaction—from hearing about or imagining someone else's actions. A girl can experience *vicarious* thrills from hearing about a friend's wild date, and people can experience *vicarious* trauma by watching too much news coverage of a grotesque disaster.

> **Fiction allows us to slide into these other heads, these other places, and look out through other eyes. And then in the tale we stop before we die, or we die** vicariously **and unharmed, and in the world beyond the tale we turn the page or close the book, and we resume our lives.**
>
> —Neil Gaiman in *American Gods*

There is also a legal concept of *vicarious* liability, in which one person or entity is responsible for the actions of another.

> **Under the Jones Act, an employer is** vicariously **liable for the death of an employee killed aboard a drilling vessel when a co-worker's gun discharged accidentally.**
>
> —Roberto Ceniceros writing for *Business Insurance*

Visceral

Visceral means emotional or instinctual. For example, a *visceral* response is a deeply felt emotion or reaction that comes from instincts or intuition rather than logic or rational thought.

Visceral comes from a Latin root that means "internal organs." Long ago, people believed that emotions came from internal organs; at various times, the liver, the heart, and the bowels have all been described as the "seat of emotion." Because of these beliefs, *visceral* took on its current meaning in the fourteenth and fifteenth centuries. Its use in this way fell out of favor for hundreds of years but reemerged in the twentieth century, and *visceral* is used quite often to describe emotional reactions today.

> **The sheer brutality and horror in this play [*The March*] is unlike anything I've ever seen on stage or in movies, and knowing**

**that there is more truth than fiction in this
work makes the impact devastating. I was
in no way prepared for the relentless
assault on my ears, the** visceral **fear I felt
when the guards were near me and the
sheer weight of bleakness that now presses
on my heart.**

—Kate Watson writing for *The Coast* (Halifax)

Visceral is also still used in medicine to describe internal organs. For example, *visceral* fat is fat that accumulates around the organs in your trunk.

Waft

A wafter guarded ships in a convoy, seeing them safely over the seas as they were propelled by their sails. **Waft** is derived from the earlier *wafter* through a process called "back formation."

Back formations arise when the original word resembles words that have a shorter root, even though the word in question doesn't come from such a root. For example, *burgle* is a back

formation from *burglar*. Just as people joke that *gruntled* should be a word for happiness because *disgruntled* means unhappy, sometime in the 1600s people decided that if runners run and singers sing, then *wafters* must *waft*. (Another example of a back formation is *edit*, which comes from *editor*.)

From the sense of a wafter flowing over the water, came the meaning of *waft* that is most common today: something that travels or floats through the air. Smells and sounds are often described as *wafting*.

> **Yon meat, 'tis sweet as summer's** wafting
> **breeze.**
>
> —Doris Grau voicing Doris Freedman (aka Lunch
> Lady Doris) in the TV show *The Simpsons*

Waft can also be used more figuratively, for example, to describe emotions:

> **You literally could see the news** waft
> **row-by-row through the mostly white**
> **crowd: "Martin Luther King's been shot.**
> **They say he's dead."**
>
> —Jim Galloway writing for the *The Atlanta Journal-
> Constitution*

Wane

To **wane** is to decrease or become smaller. A *waning* moon decreases in size, and a man of *waning* power is becoming less important.

> **My unhealthy affection for my second daughter has** waned**. Now I despise all my seven children equally.**
>
> —Evelyn Waugh

Wax is the opposite of *wane* and means "to grow." A sliver moon waxes until it becomes a full moon, which then *wanes* as the cycle continues.

Wanton

Wanton comes from Old English words that meant "wanting" and "discipline," as in wanting for discipline or undisciplined.

An early use of *wanton*, which continues to this day, has strong sexual connotations: recklessly lustful, lascivious, or lewd. Originally only women were described as *wanton*, but eventually the term came to be applied equally to both sexes.

> **Bridget Jones,** wanton **sex goddess, with a very bad man between her thighs. Dad? Hi.**
>
> —Renée Zellweger playing Bridget Jones answering the phone in the movie *Bridget Jones's Diary*

Additional meanings developed later. For example, *wanton* can describe a wild, care-free (and perhaps racy) party or a reckless, senseless crime.

Wanton

The thought of him got to preying upon me every night; I could not get rid of it. I could not drive it away, the taking of that unoffending life seemed such a wanton **thing. And it seemed an epitome of war; that all war must be just that—the killing of strangers against whom you feel no personal animosity; strangers whom, in other circumstances, you would help if you found them in trouble, and who would help you if you needed it.**

—Mark Twain in *A Private History of a Campaign That Failed*

Winnow

Winnow was originally the act of blowing air to separate grain from lighter, undesirable parts such as chaff and dirt, and *winnow* comes from the Old English word for "wind."

According to the *Oxford English Dictionary*, the first known metaphorical use of *winnow* to describe generally separating good from bad appeared in a book now know as the Wycliffe Bible. In the Middle Ages, John Wycliffe defied the Catholic Church by translating the Bible into English so it could be read by common people. Because it was one of the earliest books written in English to be widely distributed, the Wycliffe Bible played an important role in the development of the language.

> **Skeptical scrutiny is the means, in both science and religion, by which deep thoughts can be** winnowed **from deep nonsense.**
>
> —Carl Sagan

Zeitgeist

Zeitgeist comes to English directly from German in which *zeit* means "time" and *geist* means "spirit," so the *zeitgeist* is the spirit of the times—what's on people's minds or the prevailing attitudes of the age.

The search engine company Google puts together a report they call "Zeitgeist" that lists the top search terms for each year. By seeing what people are looking for online, you can get a very real insight into the spirit of the times, especially in entertainment. In 2002, people wanted to know about Spider-Man, Shakira, and the Winter Olympics. In 2010, it was Chat Roulette, the iPad, and Justin Bieber.

Because nouns are capitalized in German, *zeitgeist* is sometimes capitalized in English; it is acceptable to write it either way—uppercase or lowercase.

> **Judging [for literary awards] is a fraught business, subject to whims, biases, conflicts of interest, flickers in the** zeitgeist**, politics and relationships among jurors.**
>
> —Martin Levin writing for *The Globe and Mail*

Acknowledgments

Thank you to Emily Rothschild, who was my editor when this book began, and Beata Santora, who was my editor when this book was finished; my agent, Laurie Abkemeier; and Lisa Senz at St. Martin's who suggested this project. Thank you also to the many people who suggested words for this book, including my husband, Patrick, who made ridiculous suggestions (such as "woof") that made me laugh when I was having trouble making decisions.

I feel especially indebted to the writers whose quotations I used in this book to illustrate the meaning of each word. I spent significant time searching for ideal quotations, and when I found each one, I got a little burst of joy. It takes particular skill and care to use words as well as they did.

For etymology and definition research, my main sources were the *Oxford English Dictionary* (online edition), *Webster's Third*

Acknowledgments

New International Dictionary (online edition), and Dictionary .com. Although I did use other sources, my first stops when searching for quotations were GoodReads.com, Google News, and Wordnik.com. Without such compilations, finding excellent quotations would have been a daunting task.

About the Author

Mignon Fogarty is the creator of Quick and Dirty Tips. Formerly a magazine writer, technical writer, and entrepreneur, she has a B.A. in English from the University of Washington in Seattle and an M.S. in biology from Stanford University. She lives in Reno, Nevada. Visit her Web site at quickanddirtytips.com and sign up for the free e-mail grammar tips and free podcast.

Quick and Dirty Tips™

Helping you do things better.

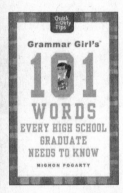

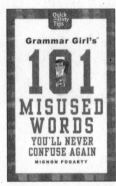

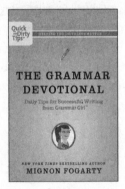

www.quickanddirtytips.com